McDonnell Douglas F-4E Phantom II

JP Vieira

Introduction

The aim of this book is to present some interesting profiles of F-4E Phantoms.

Naturally a selection had to be made, and this followed the criteria of presenting the most eye-catching or unusual schemes, and to include the greatest possible variation of the style of colours worn.

As such, examples of testing, experimental, operational, commemorative and 'shark-mouth' colour schemes are presented, which we hope will be of interest to the aviation enthusiast in general, and the scale modeller in particular. Although detailed captions will accompany each image, we feel that some extra information would be helpful for the aircraft presented; as this information would take more than the space permitted for the caption, we will present it here.

This information follows the order of the images in the book.

The McDonnell Douglas F-4E Phantom

The McDonnell Douglas F-4 Phantom II is a twin-engine, two-seat, supersonic jet fighter aircraft originally developed for the United States Navy (USN), entering service in 1960.

The United States Air Force (USAF) showed interested in the aircraft and borrowed two US Navy Phantoms, using them with the temporary designation F-110A Spectre. With the tri-service unification of aircraft designations in 1962, the naval version was termed the F-4B and the USAF version, the F-4C.

The first USAF Phantom made its maiden flight on 27 May 1963. Making its first flight on 1 August 1965, the E variant featured an integral M61 Vulcan cannon, AN/APQ-120 radar, and J79-GE-17 engines.

Later built aircraft featured slats on the wing leading edges. The E variant is the most numerous Phantom with 1,370 examples built.

Besides service with the USAF, the E variant was also exported to other countries and licence-built in Japan as the F-4EJ.

Notes on the colour schemes and markings

When developing the cannon-armed variant of the Phantom several aircraft played key roles; the first internally gun-equipped phantom was actually the RF-4C prototype, serial 62-12200 with the installation of a M61A1 gun into the nose space usually destined for reconnaissance equipment.

One of the prototypes for the cannon-armed phantom variant (YF-4E) 65-0713, was a modified F-4D aircraft. This particular aircraft was used in many testing roles and had a long career at Edwards AFB. It displayed a shark-mouth with at least two different designs; the one presented here was seen around the late 1970s.

To create the dedicated variant of the F-4E for the suppression of enemy defences, a production aircraft was modified with the installation of new electronic equipment and other alterations. Externally the aircraft had a new configuration of under-nose pod (replacing the gun with special equipment), a fin blister and an array of new antennae. The prototype of the F-4G variant, 69-7254, had areas of Day-Glo during its test period but retained overall standard SEA colours and pattern.

On the introduction of the Phantom into *Luftwaffe's* service, the F-4Fs used the standard "Norm 72" colour scheme. This was found to have serious disadvantages in the air-defence role, making the aircraft very difficult to conceal from enemy eyes. As such a series of experimental colours were trialled before the following "Norm 81" and "Norm 90" were adopted. In the book we present two of these, the so called *Weiße Milchkuh* (white milk cow) and *Maikäfer* (maize beetle).

Both the new Norm 81 and the later Norm 90 were the result of several of these experimental colour schemes; several aircraft were painted in diverse colour finishes before a standard of colours and pattern was settled upon. A similar process occurred before the creation of the Norm 83 colour scheme used on the *Luftwaffe's* RF-4E aircraft.

Japanese Phantoms operated in two main colour schemes and also displayed frequently very conspicuous colours with patches of blue, green and red applied to the baseline scheme. These latter markings were often applied to machines used in dissimilar air combat training (DACT). These markings seem to have two objectives: to make the aircraft more visible, and/or to represent the silhouette of other aircraft; aircraft tasked with target towing duties also sported special markings, either white and Day-Glo colours or large Day-Glo stripes on top of the operational colour scheme. Besides these special schemes, JASDF Phantom sported several other types of colours, namely when attending annual fighter meets; these schemes consisted of either splinter, disruptive or other pattern camouflages consisting of various shades of grey and blue (and in some rarer cases, brown and green).

Applying a shark mouth design to aircraft is a practice dating back to the very earliest years of military aviation.

There are obvious aircraft that, due to the nose shape, present themselves as particularly suitable to the application of such markings; the gun-armed F-4E is an obvious example, and that practice was followed by almost all of its operators. In varying degrees several of the operators of the F-4E Phantom applied shark (or other beasts') mouths to those aircraft.

In our selection of those marking we wish to present those most visually striking, and some lesser known examples of the practice.

Some of those marking are not of sharks' mouths but other creatures such as dragons (USAF's 512th TFS) or felines (such as the *Luftwaffe's* RF-4E of AG52), for instance.

As was the case with shark mouths, the application of special commemorative colour schemes was a practice that varied much among F-4E operators; in one extreme, operators such as the *Luftwaffe* and the JASDF employed many examples of these schemes, and on the other, some operators did not present any example of the F-4 in special, colourful finishes at all.

We believe that we could not have chosen a more suitable aircraft to conclude this presentation than one of the Thunderbirds' machines.

Throughout the research for this book, many aviation enthusiasts have helped me by sharing lesser-known photos and information. To all those people – thank you.

1

McDonnell F-4D-28-MC Phantom II s/n 65-0713.

Air Force Test Center (AFTC)/ 412th Test Wing Edwards Air Force Base, California, USA 1977.

Colour scheme used by 412th TW aircraft of overall Insignia White (FS17875) and Insignia Red (FS11136).

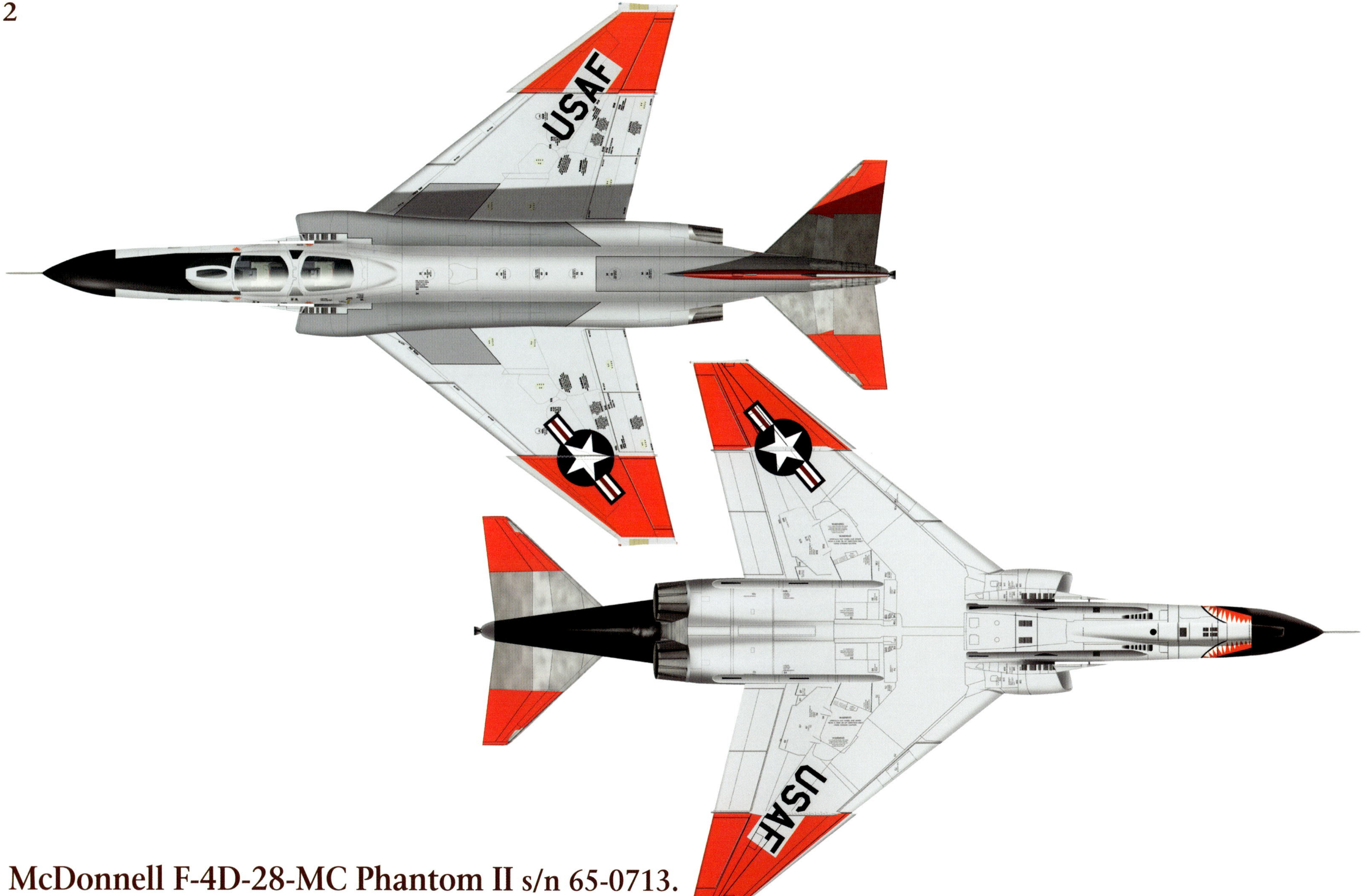

McDonnell F-4D-28-MC Phantom II s/n 65-0713.

3

McDonnell Douglas F-4E-43-MC Phantom II s/n 69-7254.

McDonnell Douglas F-4G prototype.

Edwards Air Force Base, California, USA 1975.

Standard South-East Asia colours and camouflage pattern: overall Dark Tan (FS 30219) with disruptive pattern of Medium Green (FS34102) and Dark Green (FS34079) (upper fuselage and wings) with Light Grey (FS36622) undersides. Areas of Fluorescent Red – FS28913/ Day-Glo (fin, wing-tips).

McDonnell Douglas F-4E-43-MC Phantom II s/n 69-7254.

McDonnell Douglas F-4E-43-MC Phantom II s/n 69-7254.

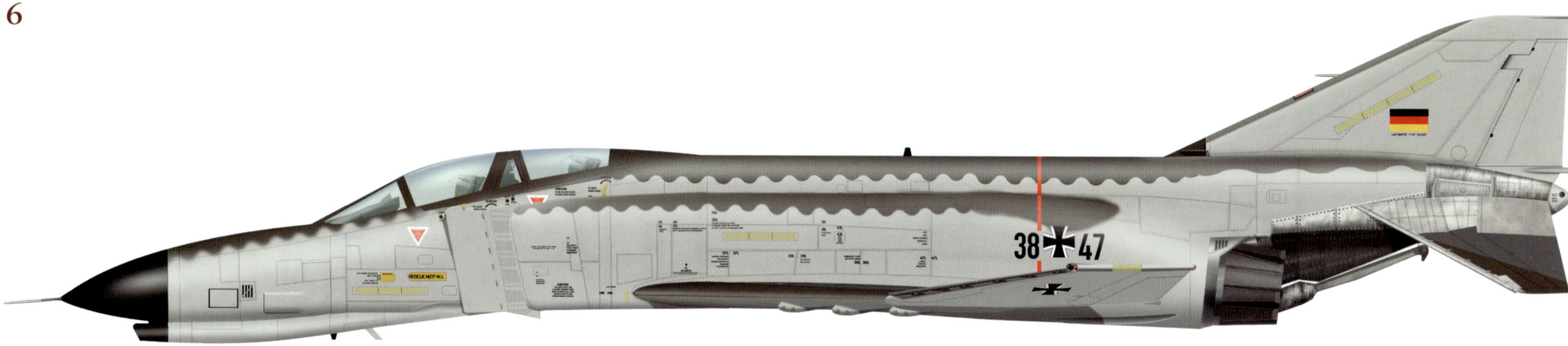

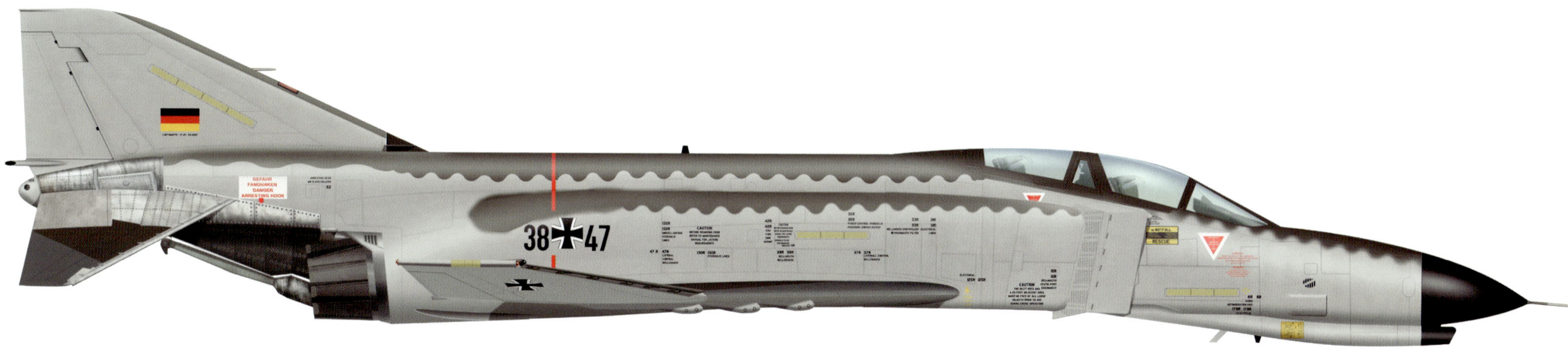

McDonnell Douglas F-4F-59-MC Phantom II s/n 72-1257 – 38+47.

JG 71 "Richthofen" Wittmundhafen Air Base, Lower Saxony, Germany 1980.

Weiße Milchkuh scheme. Overall *Lichtgrau* RAL 7035 (Light Grey) with new disruptive pattern of *Basaltgrau* RAL 7012 (Basalt Grey) and *Gelboliv* RAL 6014 (Yellow Olive). Upper wings and stabiliser with Norm 72 colours: *Basaltgrau* RAL 7012 (Basalt Grey) and geometric pattern of *Gelboliv* RAL 6014 (Yellow Olive).

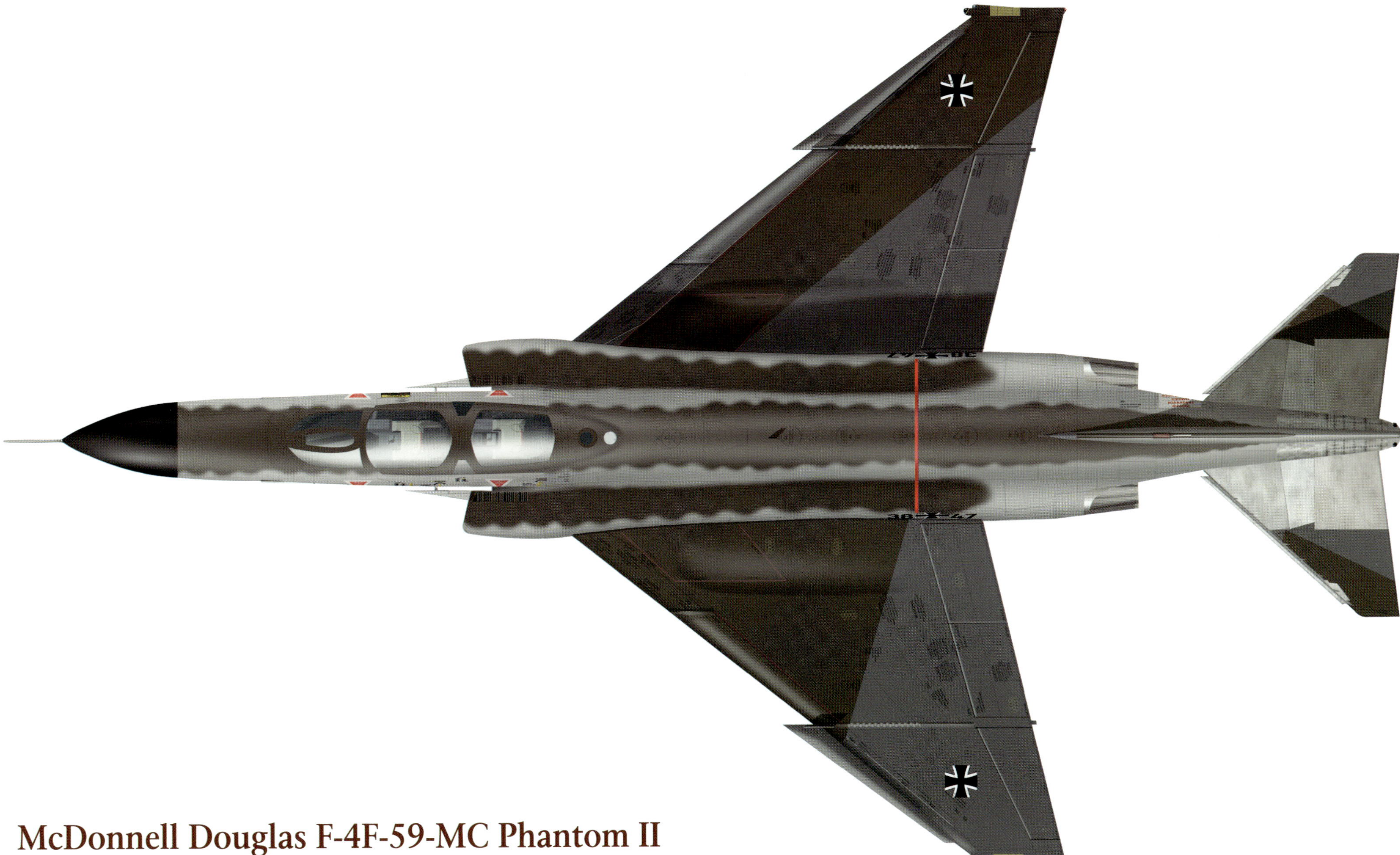

McDonnell Douglas F-4F-59-MC Phantom II
s/n 72-1257 – 38+47.

McDonnell Douglas F-4F-59-MC Phantom II
s/n 72-1257 – 38+47.

9

McDonnell Douglas F-4F-52-MC Phantom II s/n 72-1117 – 37+07.

JG 74 "Mölders" Neuburg Air Base, Bavaria, Germany.

Maikäfer scheme. Overall Grey (mixture of *Lichtgrau* RAL 7035 – Light Grey – and *Silbergrau* RAL 7001 – Silver Grey) and disruptive pattern of *Basaltgrau* RAL7012 (Basalt Grey), *Gelboliv* RAL 6014 (Yellow Olive) and *Tiefschwarz* RAL 9005 (Jet Black)

McDonnell Douglas F-4F-52-MC Phantom II
s/n 72-1117 – 37+07.

McDonnell Douglas F-4F-52-MC Phantom II
s/n 72-1117 – 37+07.

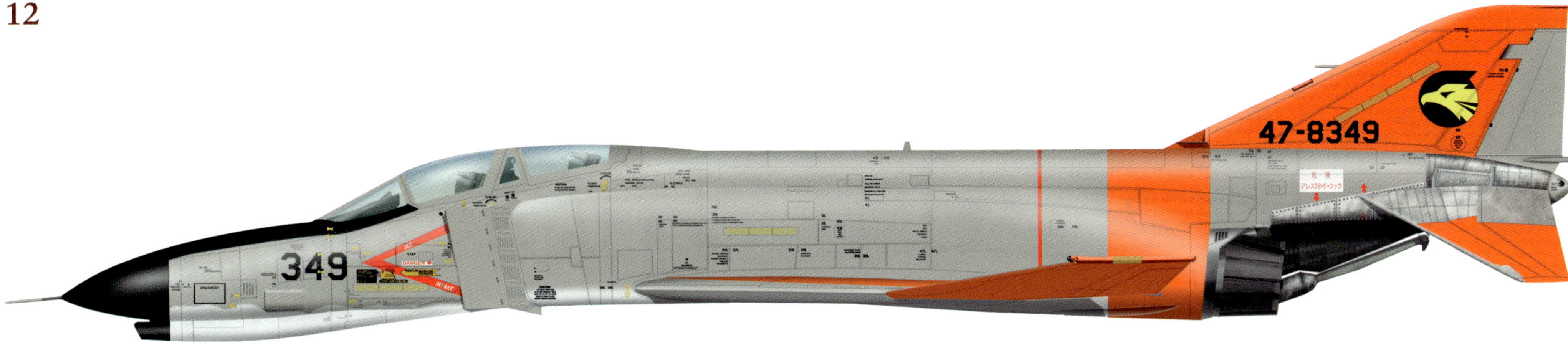

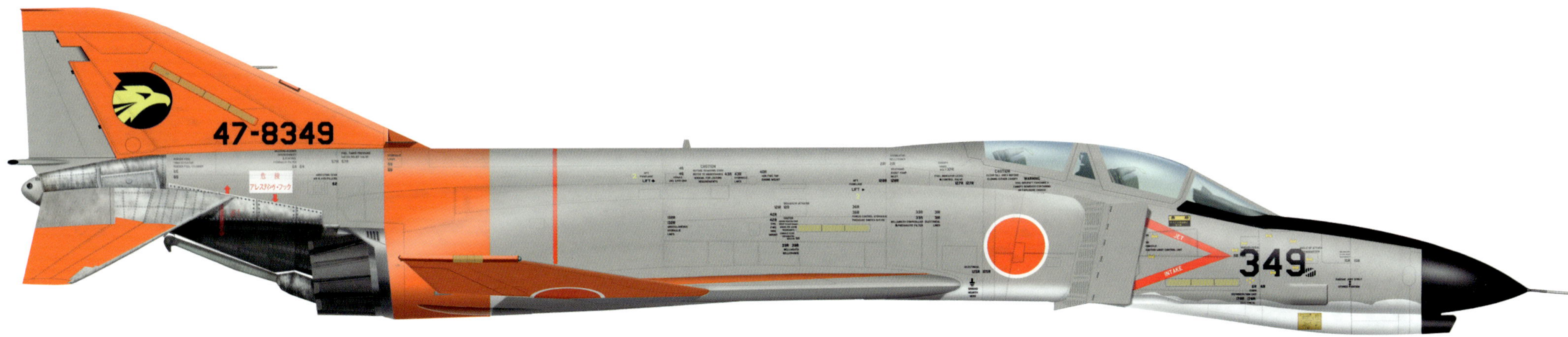

McDonnell Douglas/Mitsubishi F-4EJ Phantom II 47-8349.

306th Squadron, Komatsu 1981.

JASDF F-4EJ Phantom's first colour scheme: overall Grey (FS16440) with Insignia White (FS17875) undersides.

Areas of FS28913 (Fluorescent Red – Day-Glo).

McDonnell Douglas/Mitsubishi F-4EJ
Phantom II 47-8349.

14

McDonnell Douglas/Mitsubishi F-4EJ Phantom II 17-8438.

305th Squadron, Hyakuri 1992.

Temporary colour scheme of overall Pale Blue (FS35526) with disruptive areas of Medium Blue (FS35190).

McDonnell Douglas/Mitsubishi F-4EJ Phantom II 17-8438.

McDonnell Douglas/Mitsubishi F-4EJ Phantom II 17-8438.

17

McDonnell Douglas F-4E-40-MC Phantom II s/n 68-0480.

512th Tactical Fighter Squadron/86th Tactictal Fighter Group, Ramstein Air Base, Germany 1983.

Wraparound South-East Asia (SEA) colours and camouflage pattern: baseline Tan with disruptive pattern of Forest Green and Dark Green extending to the undersurfaces Tan (FS 30219)/ Forest Green (FS 34102)/ Dark Green (FS 34079).

McDonnell Douglas F-4E-40-MC Phantom II s/n 68-0480.

McDonnell Douglas F-4E-40-MC Phantom II s/n 68-0480.

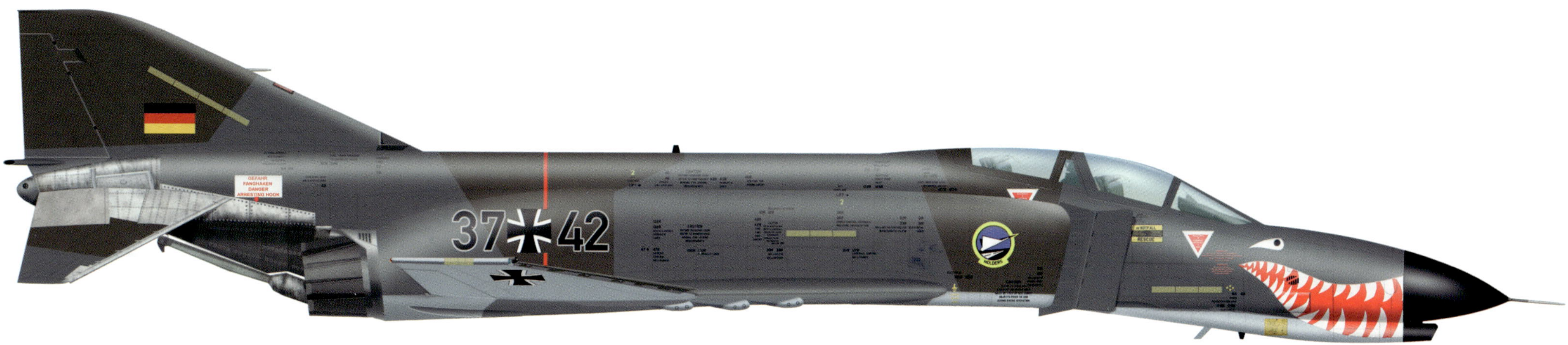

McDonnell Douglas F-4F-54-MC Phantom II s/n 72-1152.

JG 74 "Mölders", Neuburg Air Base, Bavaria, Germany 1982.

Norm 72 colours and pattern: *Basaltgrau* RAL 7012 (Basalt Grey) and geometric pattern of *Gelboliv* RAL 6014 (Yellow Olive), *Weissaluminium* RAL 9006 (White Aluminium) undersides.

McDonnell Douglas F-4F-54-MC Phantom II s/n 72-1152.

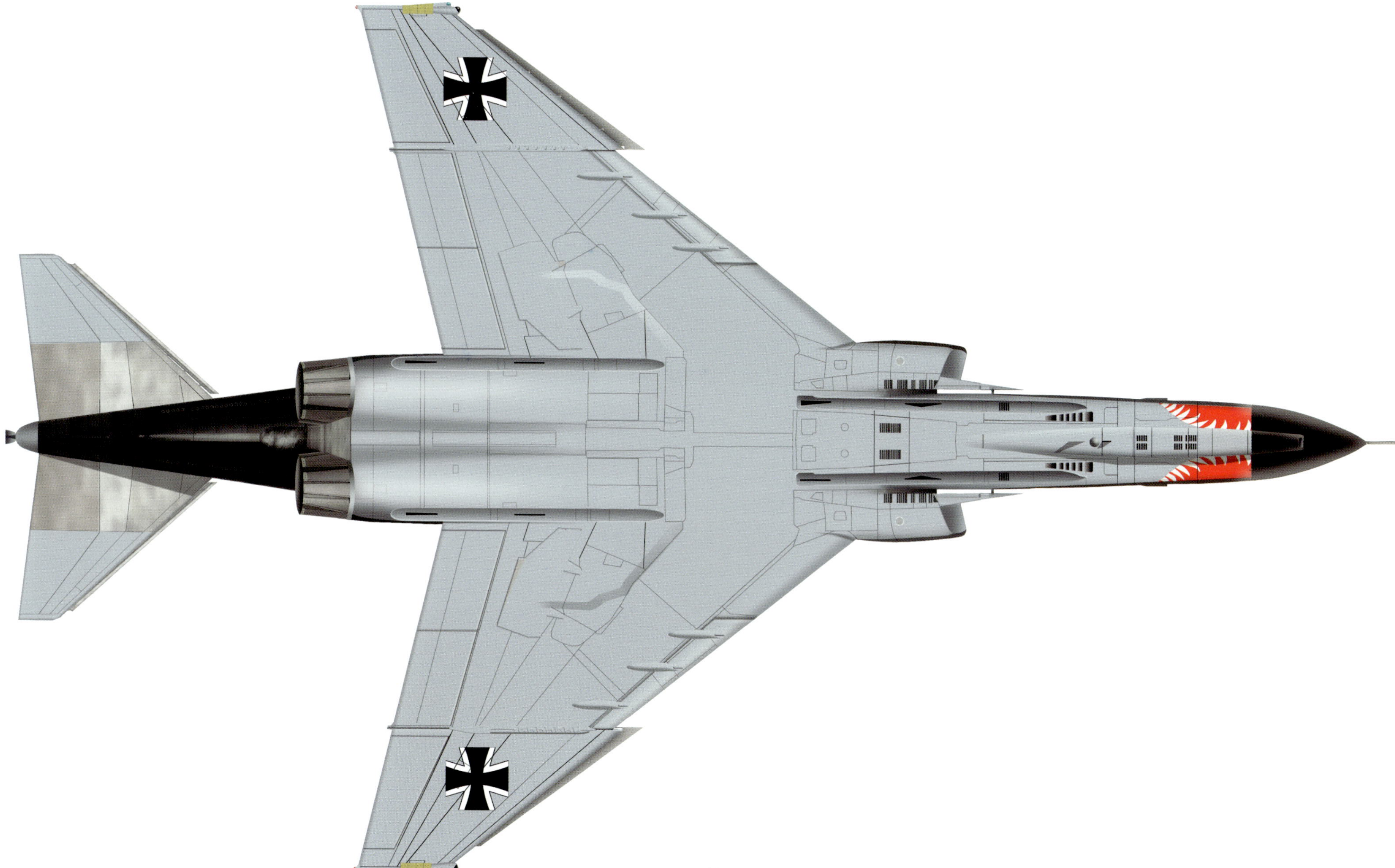

McDonnell Douglas F-4F-54-MC Phantom II s/n 72-1152.

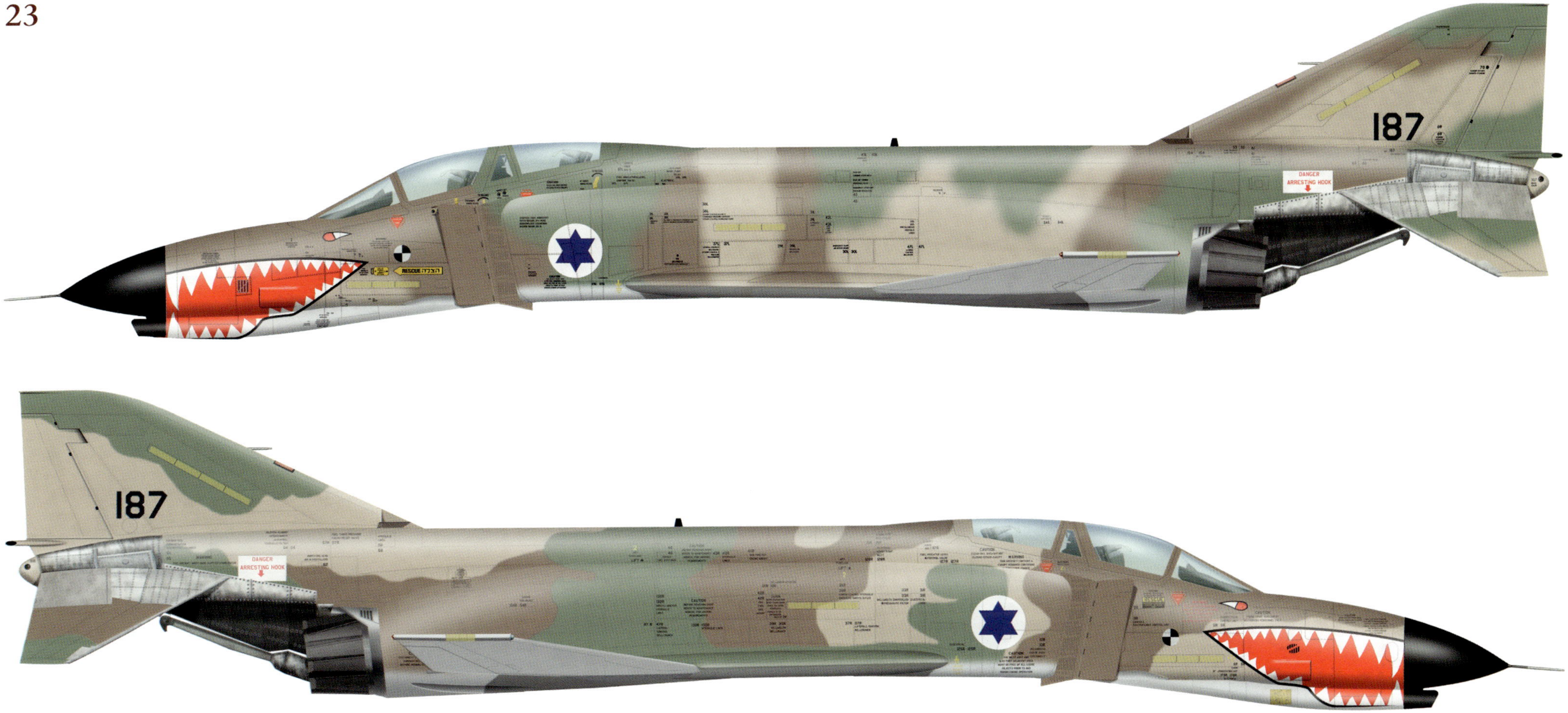

McDonnell F-4E-41-MC Phantom II F-4E Kurnass s/n 68-0544 – 187.

69th Squadron "The Hammers" Hatzerim Air Base, Israel 1971.

Baseline Tan (FS33531) with disruptive pattern of Brown (FS30219) and Pale Green (FS34227) with Light Compass Ghost Grey (FS36375).

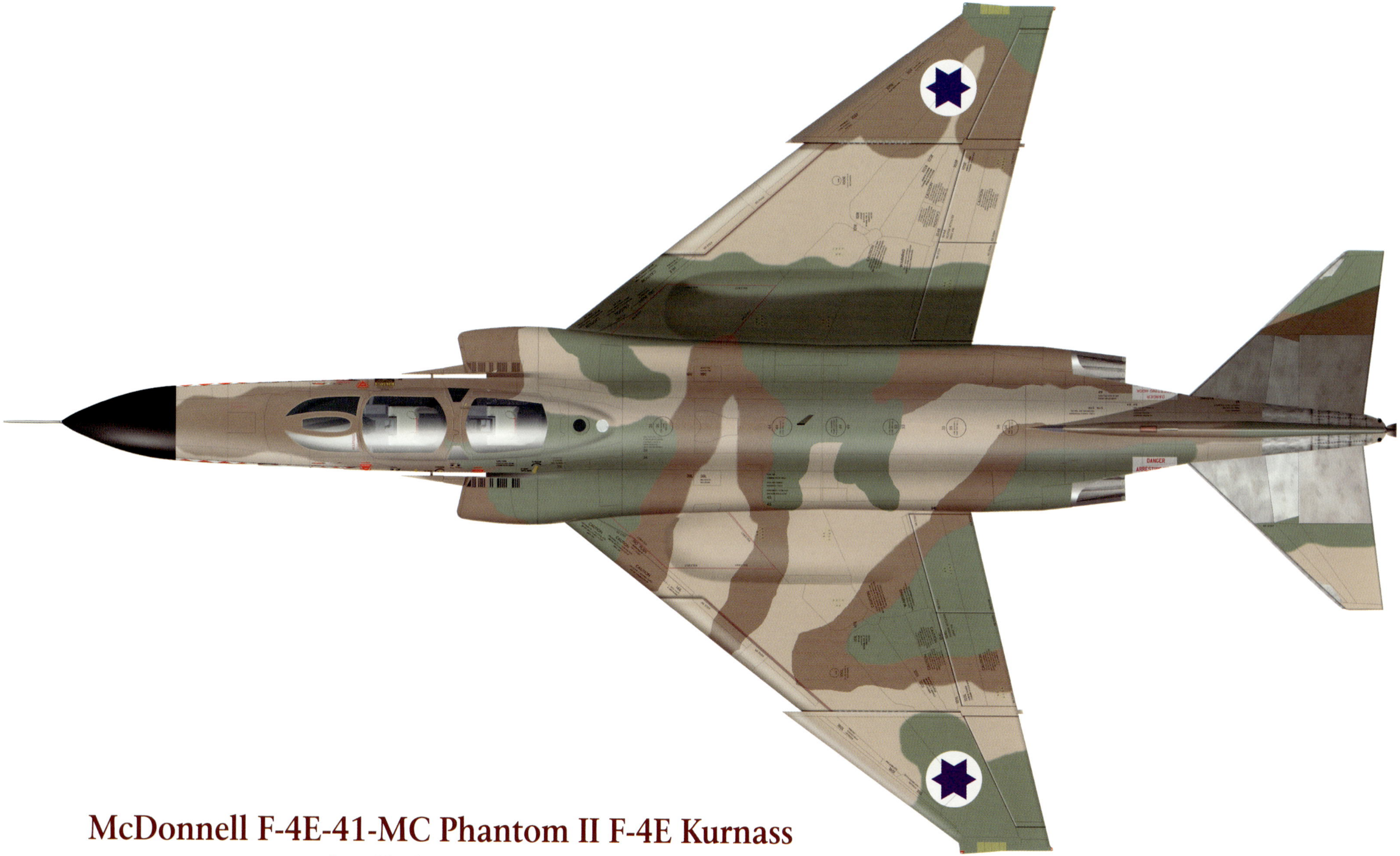

McDonnell F-4E-41-MC Phantom II F-4E Kurnass
s/n 68-0544 – 187.

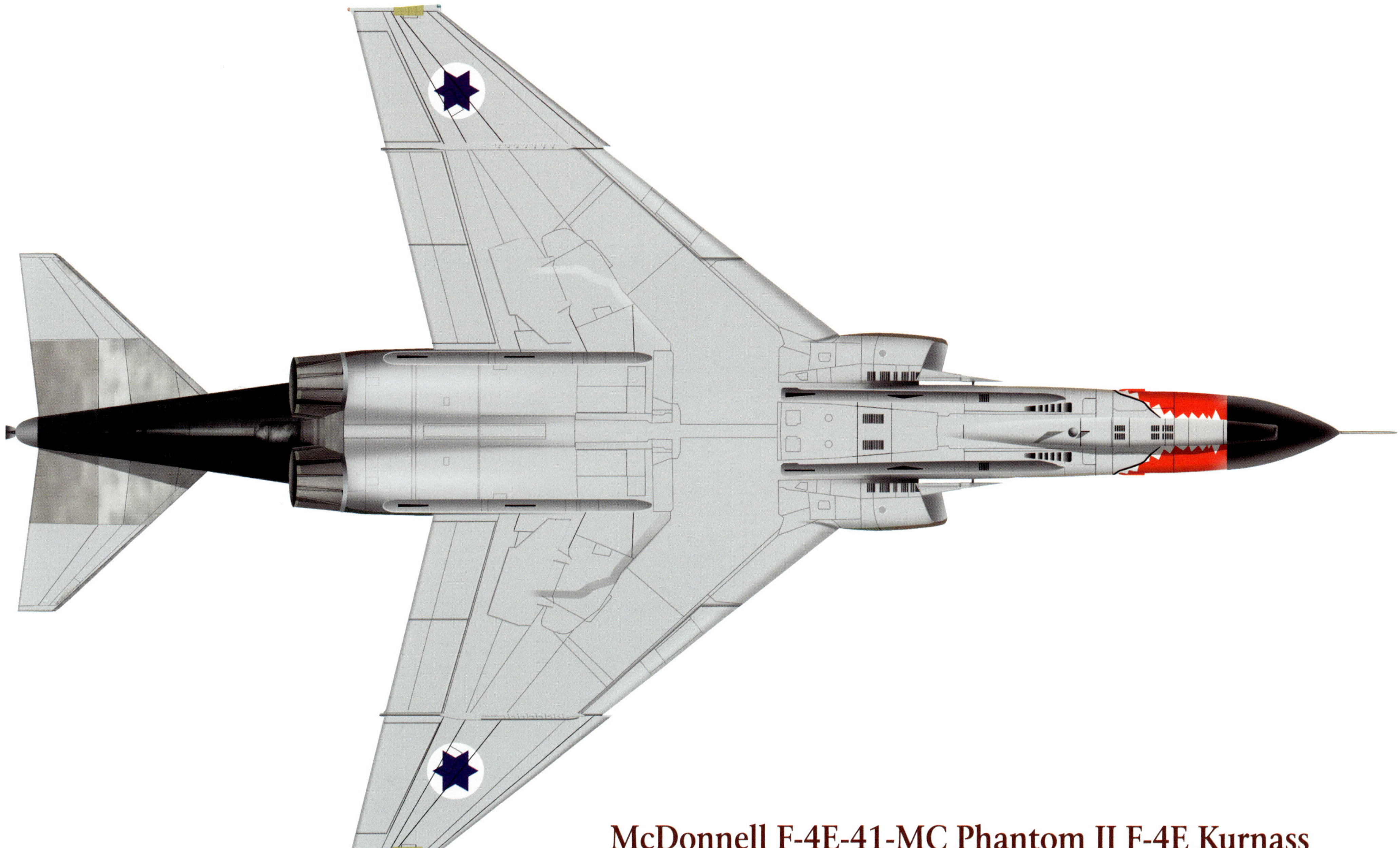

McDonnell F-4E-41-MC Phantom II F-4E Kurnass
s/n 68-0544 – 187.

McDonnell Douglas F-4E-58-MC Phantom II, F-4E-2020 Terminator s/n 73-1046.

111 *Filo* (Squadron) "Panthers", Eskişehir Air Base, Turkey 2014.

Overall Medium Grey (FS26270) with areas of Dark Grey (FS26118).

McDonnell Douglas F-4E-58-MC Phantom II,
F-4E-2020 Terminator s/n 73-1046.

McDonnell Douglas F-4E-58-MC Phantom II,
F-4E-2020 Terminator s/n 73-1046.

McDonnell Douglas RF-4E-46-MC Phantom II, F-4F Phantom II s/n 69-7499 – 35+52.

AG 52, Leck Air Base, Schleswig-Holstein, Germany1994.

Overall *Tiefschwarz* RAL 9005 (Jet Black).

McDonnell Douglas RF-4E-46-MC Phantom II,
F-4F Phantom II s/n 69-7499 – 35+52.

McDonnell Douglas/Mitsubishi F-4EJ Kai, Phantom II 07-8435.

301st Hitokai (Squadron), Hyakuri 2003.

Special scheme of overall White with areas of Black, Red and Blue.

McDonnell Douglas/Mitsubishi F-4EJ Kai
Phantom II 07-8435.

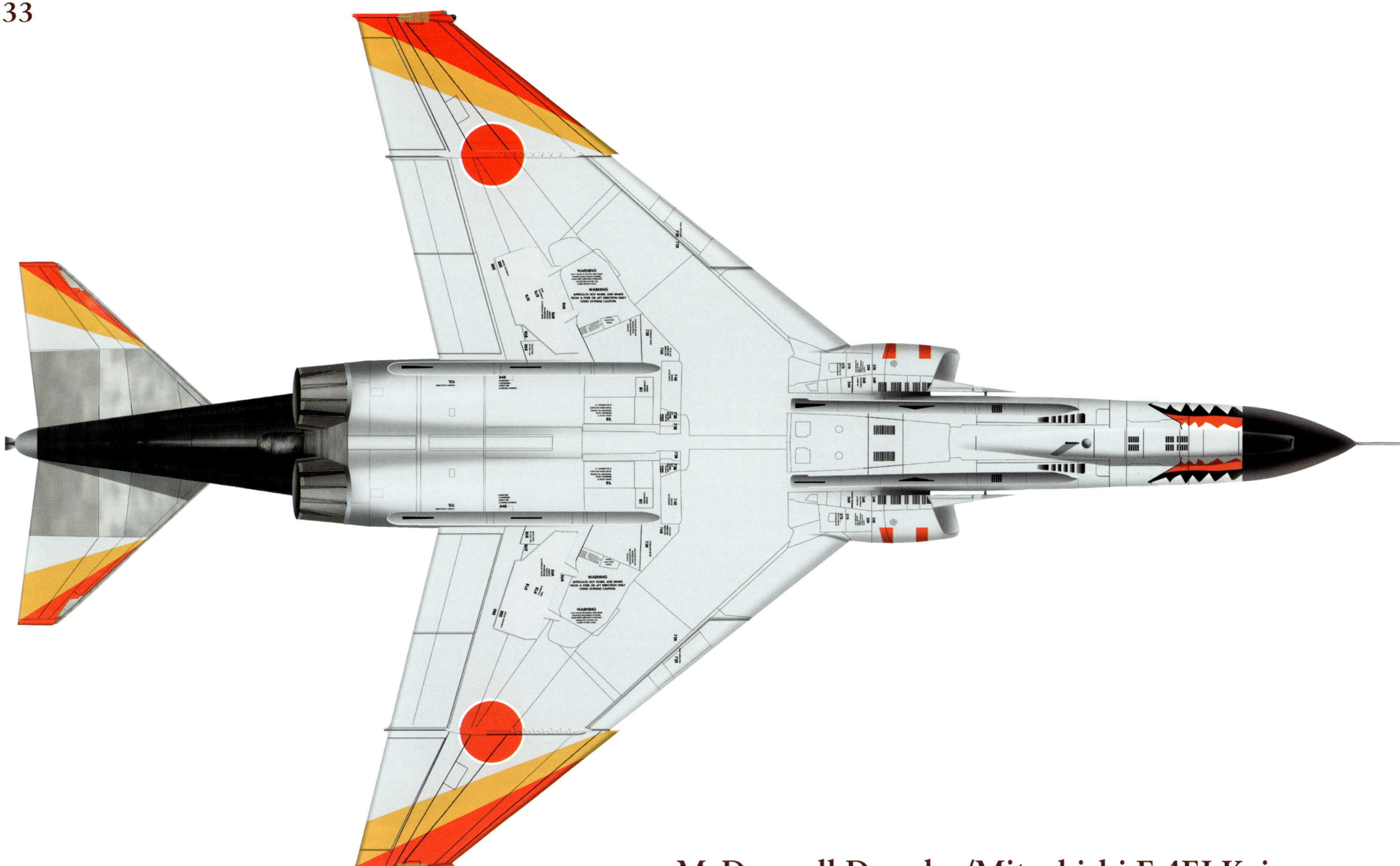

McDonnell Douglas/Mitsubishi F-4EJ Kai
Phantom II 07-8435.

McDonnell Douglas RF-4E-43-MC Phantom II s/n 69-7450 – 7450.

348 MTA (Squadron), Larissa AB, Greece 2013.

Norm 83A colours and pattern: RAL 6003 *Olivgrün* (Olive Green), RAL7021 *Schwarzgrau* (Black Grey) and FS34079 *Waldgrün* (Leaf Green).

Special commemorative scheme with the colours of the 348 MTA emblem of Green and Yellow.

McDonnell Douglas RF-4E-43-MC Phantom II
s/n 69-7450 – 7450.

McDonnell Douglas RF-4E-43-MC Phantom II
s/n 69-7450 – 7450.

McDonnell Douglas F-4F-58-MC Phantom II – 72-1247 – 38+37.

JG 72 "Westfalen", Rheine-Hopsten Air Base, North-Rhine Westphalia, Germany 2001.

Special colour scheme of *Feuerrot* RAL3000 (Flame Red), *Tiefschwarz* RAL9005 (Jet Black) and *Chromgelb* RAL1007 (Daffodil Yellow) with *Gelb* RAL 1028 (Gold) undersides.

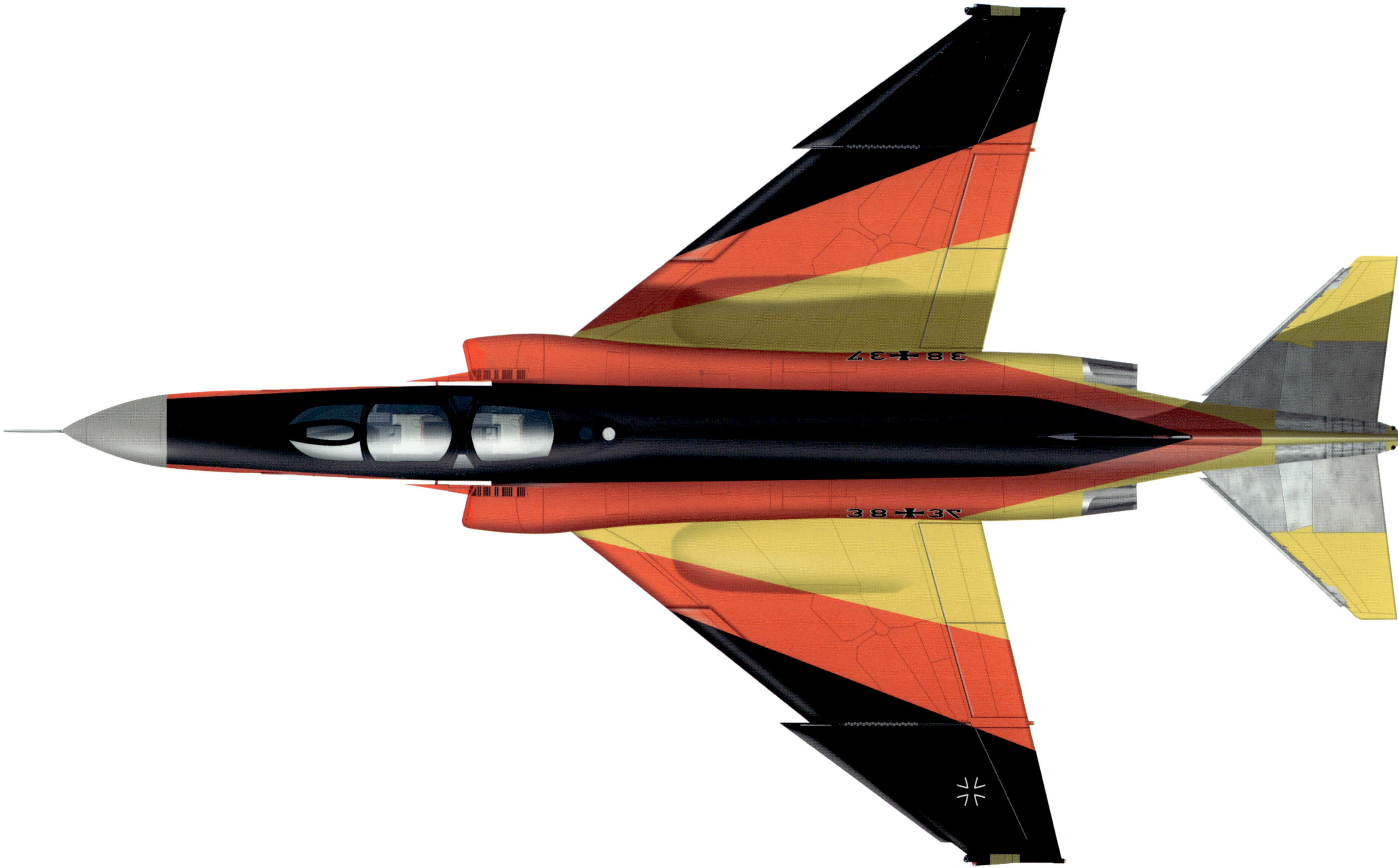

McDonnell Douglas F-4F-58-MC Phantom II – 72-1247 – 38+37.

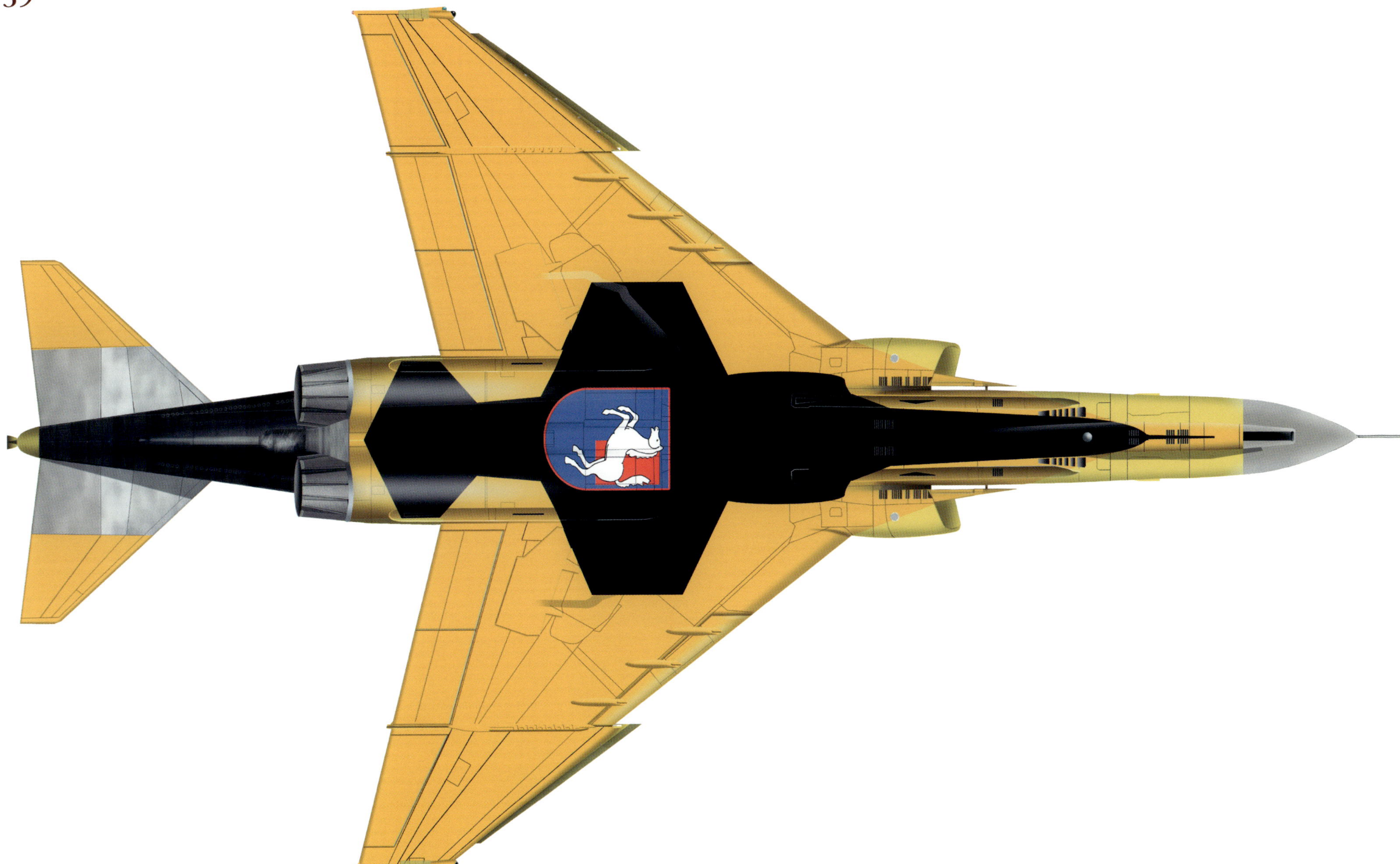

McDonnell Douglas F-4F-58-MC Phantom II – 72-1247 – 38+37.

McDonnell F-4E-33-MC Phantom II 66-0377 – "1".

USAF Air Demonstration Squadron – "Thunderbirds", Nellis Air Force Base, Nevada, USA 1973.

Thunderbirds colour scheme: Insignia White (FS17875), Insignia Blue (FS15044), and Insignia Red (FS11136).

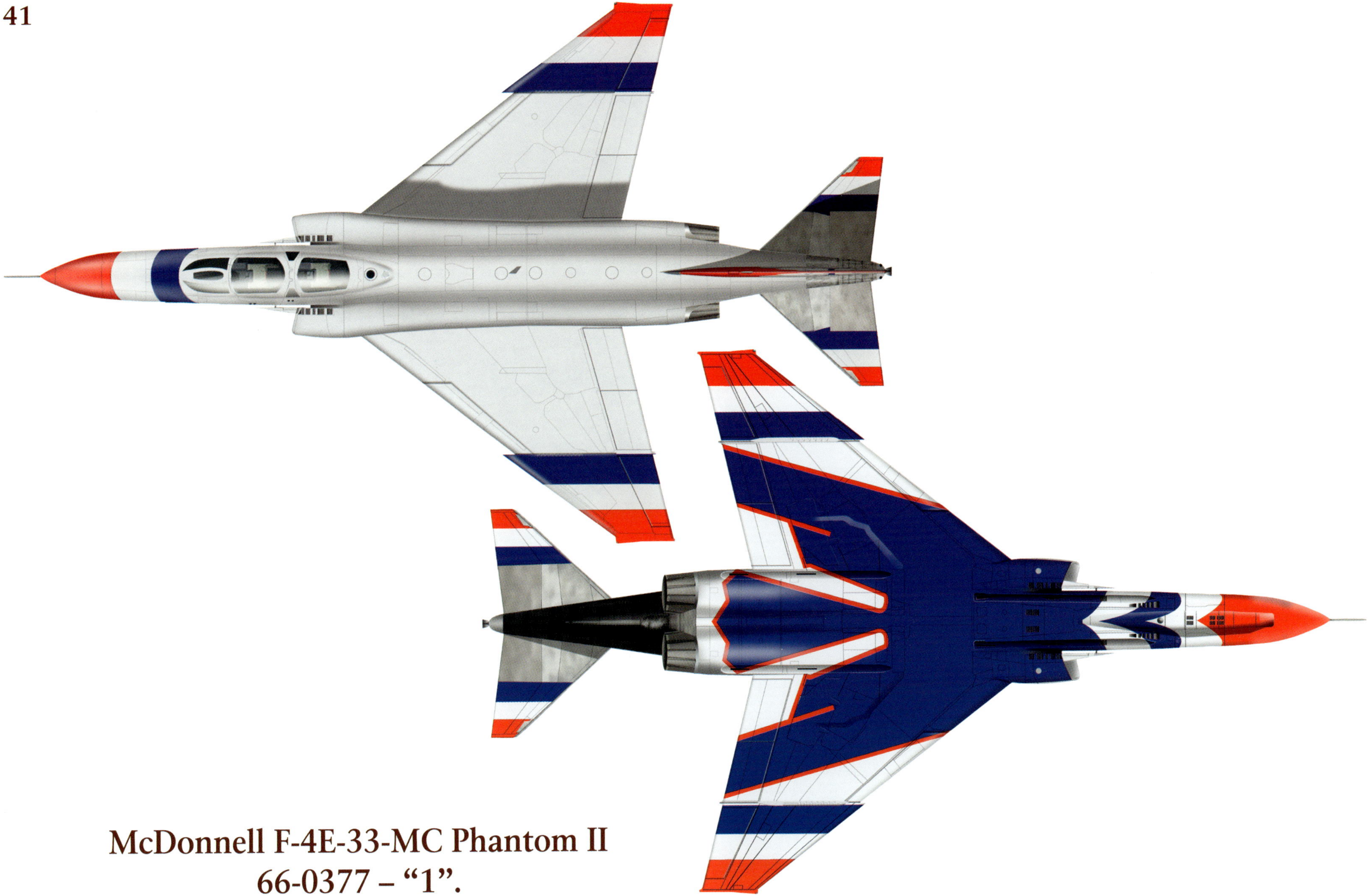

McDonnell F-4E-33-MC Phantom II
66-0377 – “1”.

Published in Poland in 2017
by STRATUS sp. j.
Po. Box 123,
27-600 Sandomierz 1, Poland
e-mail: office@stratusbooks.pl
for
MMPBooks,
3 Gloucester Close,
Petersfield,
Hampshire GU32 3AX
e-mail: office@mmpbooks.biz

ISBN 978-83-65281-33-3

Editor in chief
Roger Wallsgrove

Editorial Team
Bartłomiej Belcarz
Robert Pęczkowski
Artur Juszczak

Colour profiles
JP Vieira

DTP
Artur Juszczak

Printed by
Drukarnia Diecezjalna,
ul. Żeromskiego 4,
27-600 Sandomierz
www.wds.pl
marketing@wds.pl

PRINTED IN POLAND

Also in this series.